Emotional Intelligence:

Build Self-Awareness to Achieve Breakthrough Success

Aya Chante

Table Of Contents

Your Free Gift

As a way of saying thanks for your purchase, Aya has made a Free companion to this book that will help you get results with regards to your purpose, finances, health and many more using the power of affirmations. Get excited, enthusiastic, and live a more fulfilling life with: *101 Affirmations Companion Guide.*

This PDF has **actionable and easy to do techniques** in a printable checklist to get the results you want.

http://bit.ly/affirmpdf

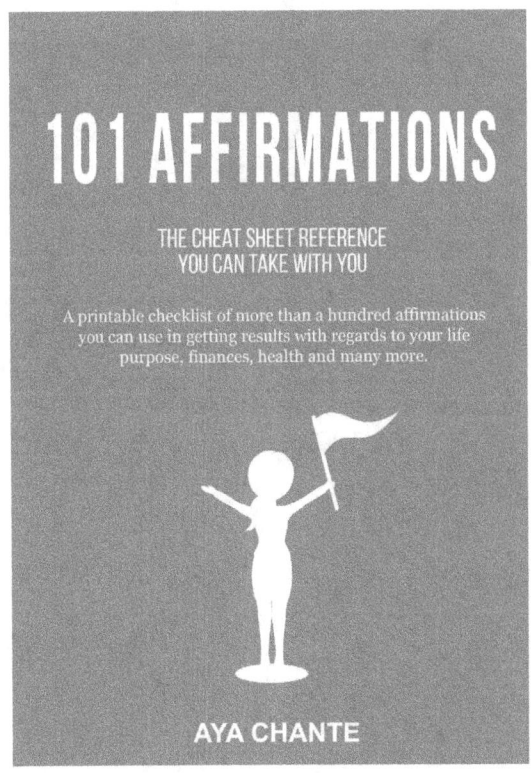

INTRODUCTION

Introduction

I want to thank you and congratulate you for downloading the book "Emotional Intelligence: Build self-awareness to achieve breakthrough success".

This book contains proven steps and strategies on how to become a truly successful person by building, developing and using your emotional intelligence. Everyone struggles with relationships, work and achieving personal goals, but you don't have to. You can make the path to what you want easier and more enjoyable by developing a set of skills associated with emotional intelligence.

Here's an inescapable fact: you will need to know how your emotions and other people's emotions work if you want to get ahead in life. It's not enough to have logic and facts on your side. People are influenced most profoundly by other people, and it takes a deep understanding of how our emotions work to understand people on that level. You can be the one influencing and guiding the course of your life with the information in this book.

If you do not develop your emotional intelligence, you may find yourself in the same spot you are in now, only ten or twenty years down the line. Too many people make the same mistakes over and over again. Don't blame your failure on others- take charge of your path.

It's time for you to become a truly emotionally intelligent person. Studies have shown that emotional intelligence is linked to improved academic performance, success at work, happiness in relationships and improved sense of overall well-being. Emotional intelligence is not something written in stone. Unlike your IQ, which turns out to predict success less strongly than people usually imagine, your EQ can be developed and enhanced. The following pages will make developing the skills of emotional intelligence easy and straightforward. You'll be surprised by how much you can gain from such a simple concept.

CHAPTER 1
WHAT EMOTIONAL INTELLIGENCE IS

Chapter 1

What Emotional Intelligence Is

Definition of Emotional Intelligence

Emotional intelligence generally refers to the ability to identify your own emotions and the emotions in others, and to use that information about yours and other people's emotion to guide your actions in relationships and situations. There are four key components that define emotional intelligence.

<u>4 Core Parts of EI</u>

1. The ability to understand your own emotions- This involves being able to recognize your emotions as they occur, to label them and to even have an idea of why you are feeling them. This is associated with good intuition and decision making.

2. The ability to control your emotions- This means you are even keeled in a variety of potentially emotionally charged situations. You aren't overwhelmed by any of your emotions. It also includes a degree of self-management, meaning the ability to handle your distressing emotions so they don't cripple you. At the same time this involves the ability to marshal good emotions when you need them.

3. The ability to read emotions in others- This is basically the concept of empathy. It encompasses your ability to relate to others, step into their shoes and understand them as you might understand yourself.

4. The ability to manage relationships- This is a synthesis of the previous abilities that is critical to emotional intelligence. It depends on how well you utilize and put together the previous abilities. Without this ability, even excellence in recognize your own emotions or those of others will do you little good.

You are likely stronger in certain areas and weaker in others. Becoming aware of where you are already solid and where you need work is an important part of improving your EQ (and it can be improved- we'll explore that in more depth later).

Emotional intelligence involves a range of skills. Women tend to be better than men at empathy and related social skills. Men tend to be better at self confidence in groups and managing distressing emotions. But those differences disappear between men and women who are in the top ten percent of high achieving men and women. These people have picked up the skills they need to succeed, and so can you.

History

Emotional intelligence's greatest champion is widely considered the author and psychologist Daniel Goleman. His 1995 book on the subject gained wide popularity and made emotional intelligence a word common in our language. However, the concept of emotional intelligence goes back to at least the 60s, when it was discussed by Michael Beldoch in a paper about the communication of emotional meaning. The concept became slowly more widespread in academic and literary circles. By the late 80s the term EQ (Emotional Quotient) was beginning to be used and from the 90s on there has been more popular and scientific interest in the concept.

Difference Between IQ and EQ

Intelligence Quotient (IQ) is a score related to performance on a specific test to measure general intelligence. It was first developed in the early 1900s by a French psychologist. It has since gone under many revisions. IQ tests are scored such that the average score is about 100 and most people fall within a certain deviation of that, about 10 or 20 pints above or below. A particularly high or low score indicates either particular intelligence or some intellectual deficiency, respectively, as compared to the general population.

Stanford-Binet is a common IQ test in the United States. The Wechsler Adult Intelligence Scale (WAIS) is the most commonly used IQ test in the world. It is interesting to note that the average IQ has been slowly increasing over the past hundred years, mostly due to the increasingly cognitively demanding and engaging environment children grow up in.

EQ on the other hand shows no evidence of increasing in the general population over time. EQ stand for Emotional Quotient, though there is currently no general test to measure any Emotional Quotient. The term is mainly used to reference EI or emotional intelligence back to IQ, and suggest that just as there are some people with particularly high or low intelligence, there are people with high and low emotional intelligence. Emotional Intelligence is something that varies from person to person, but just as with IQ, there is a certain average range most people fall into.

A final important difference between IQ and EQ is that a person's IQ tends to be stable over time. That means that though you might study hard your whole life, generally your IQ does not change more than a few points over the course of your life. EQ on the other hand is something you can develop. You can improve your EQ over time. This is not something, however, that you do in a day. It might take months, but you can work on it by pinpointing those areas of your EQ that could use some development and then focusing on those areas. You can retrain your mind to think in new ways and behave in new ways.

How to Tell the Difference between EQ and IQ-an Exercise

IQ and EQ are very different but it may not be immediately clear how different. To help, we have some scenarios or situations in which either IQ or EQ is more useful. Think about which you would chose for each one and compare to the key at the end.

1. You have a big test in front of you, and it's all material that you studied. You're going to be primarily using your...

2. You just started a new job and you need to figure out how you are going to fit in amongst coworkers. You're going to be primarily using your...

3. You need to figure out how to fit all your belongings into a small truck so they all fit for your move

4. You need to judge the character of the neighborhood your moving into

5. You want to compare the pros and cons of refinancing your house

6. You want to compare the pros and cons of staying in your current romantic relationships

7. You are haggling with a street vendor

8. You're working collaboratively with a small team of people as their leader and need to have their full cooperation for success

1. IQ, 2. EQ, 3. IQ, 4. EQ, 5. IQ, 6. EQ, 7. EQ 8. EQ

CHAPTER 2
DISCOVERING YOUR EMOTIONAL QUOTIENT

Chapter 2

Discovering Your Emotional Quotient

Now that we know *what* EQ is, it's time to figure out *what* your EQ is. Remember, unlike IQ, there is no one test that you can take to receive a number for your EQ. Instead, you'll try to get a sense of your overall emotional intelligence by doing some investigations into yourself. This will involve introspection: looking inwards and learning about what you are like. It's not something that can be done in an afternoon. It will take time, but that time will be well worth the rewards your newly acquired understanding brings you.

How to Gain Self Awareness of Your Own Emotions

<u>Physically</u>

Often our emotions find expression somewhere in our body. Some people report a feeling of "hotness" as they get angry, others feel dread or sadness as a heaviness in the pit of the stomach. Some people describe happiness as a sense of lightness. Our emotions are actually full body experiences, they are not confined to just our brain. The mind-body link is real and each affects the other.

In fact, there are numerous well documented studies that have shown physical responses the body has to stress, for example. A purely mental phenomenon of say having a difficult work environment translates into things like a weakened immune system or ulcers.

So one avenue of personal investigation involves checking in with your body. As you being to pay more attention to your emotions, also pay attention to your body. Do a head to toe check: start with the top of your head and check in with various parts of your body until you reach your feet. See how everything feels.

Is your stomach in knots? Maybe you're stressed, dreading something, or anxious. Is your back, shoulders or some other body part tight and stiff? Maybe you're angry, anxious or tense. Does your whole body feel sluggish, slow tired? Maybe you are sad, despondent, hopeless. Do you feel energetic? Maybe you are happy, or maybe its anger. Each of us is unique in how our body responds and expresses emotions, but our bodies are often relatively consistent. So if you notice something physically accompany an emotion, then the next time you notice that physical feeling first it's like a hint or a cheat sheet to your emotions, giving you a heads up to what you are feeling.

Verbally

You can talk through what you are experiencing with someone else. Other people offer a unique perspective to our own problems and issues. Perhaps you have an especially empathetic friend. It's possible he/she might know what you are feeling before you do. If you don't have anyone handy you can imagine the people you would most want to talk to and walk through an imaginary conversation with them. Usually we know our friends and family well enough to get a sense of how they would react to what we would say even before we do. Even an imaginary conversation helps. In any case, talking out loud lets you work through what you are feeling.

As you struggle to put into words what you are experiencing, your mind will remember that struggle, and will associate the words you choose each time with the feeling. Soon enough, as you practice linking words and sentences to how you feel, you will find the words come quicker and easier. Eventually you will have a whole vocabulary for each emotion.

Mentally

Think back to the situation that seemed to spark your current emotion. What happened there, and what did you think when it happened? What were some of your earliest thoughts when it happened? Examining the situation as soon after the emotion becomes apparent is best as the memory of what happened and what went through your mind will be freshest.

It can even help to imagine someone else in the same situation. Pick a friend, family member, or even a relatable fictional character you identify with. What would these people be feeling in the same situation?

<u>Behaviorally</u>

What actions do you want to take? Many emotions are easily associated with certain behaviors. If for instance you want to dance on a rooftop while singing with a grin on your face, you're probably happy, or at least I would hope you are. If the emotion you are experiencing makes you want to go out and do something, anything, but do it immediately you may be angry. Anger has a strong motivational component to it. Yet, if shortly afterwards you feel tried and just want to lay down, and sleep or turn off your brain somehow then you might be sad. The progression just described is probably more common than you think. A loss may be angering at first and then as the anger dies down, the loss may be experienced as sadness, and this is normal. It's important when investigating your emotions to not become afraid or suspect of them. An attitude of curiosity is best.

Some other examples: Fear tends to induce a behavior of wanting to avoid something, withdraw from a situation and get away quickly. Shame tends to get people to quiet down, turn inward, and make themselves as hard to notice as possible. Jealousy may be like anger, but closely linked to an object of focus like a person, an item, or a characteristic.

Strengths and Weaknesses

If you find yourself frequently repeating the same refrain about some difficulty in your life, this is a good indicator it may be a point to work on. For example: "I keep going out with people who do x, and it ends poorly". Or: "I'm really good at what I do but I keep getting fired." Any pattern of problems with other people is a signal of a weakness in your emotional intelligence. This is not something to despair over, or beat yourself up over. You are lucky if you can catch it, because now you can go about improving your emotional intelligence and stop making the same mistakes.

What tends to go well for you? Think back to your experiences with other people. Can you find a theme for the types of situations or interactions that went particularly well? Maybe you tend to get along with strangers easily, or maybe you do really well with closer personal one on one conversations where people open up to you. Maybe you are the life of the party and tend to be able to convince a crowd to follow some idea. Think back to when you were really happy or successful with another person, to when things went well. Somewhere along this line of inquiry you will find hints of your strengths.

Itemize Yourself

One way to gauge your strengths and weaknesses, as well as gain more insight into your emotions and self is to sit down and write out some of these things and check back on them occasionally. Start with only a few items in a few categories like: strengths/weaknesses; goal; priorities; needs. After writing them out, leave the list alone for a short span of time from a day to a week. Come back to the list and look it over again. Does it make sense? Does it reflect you? Modify it as you see fit, then begin to use the list: work on your weaknesses, try to use strengths to your advantage, make plans for reaching your goals. Check back with your list every now and then and update it and even make it more specific when you need to, like adding short term and long term goals, or making note of things that didn't work and why you think they didn't work.

Gut Feelings?

Gut feelings are basically intuitions: a judgment about a person, thing or situation that we can't explain. These intuitions tend to seem like they come from nowhere, but they don't. They have two origins: the outside world and your inner world.

On one level, intuitions come from something you noticed in your immediate environment, but it was something that you did not consciously notice or give strong meaning to. Your mind on the other hand, has perceptual awareness, and is constantly trying to match situations around you with experiences you have had in the past. So part of that gut feeling, is when your mind, without you doing any work, is able to make that match and based on the similarity of situations, come to a decision.

Let's say for example you were in a park one day when you heard a loud cracking noise and saw a tree fall only feet in front of you. You were unhurt, but it was still a scary experience. Your mind logs that whole scenario because it was so scary. When it finds other situations that resemble that one, it will give you a warning, a gut feeling that something is not right, or that maybe you should be cautious. So back to our example, maybe you are on an old deck one day and you hear a low cracking noise. It's years later and you don't immediately think of any similar experience, but your mind does. You suddenly have an intuition that you should get away from that cracking noise, and just in time because part of the old wooden deck collapses. Your intuition comes in large part as a combination of past experience and current situation that your mind evaluates without your conscious thought.

The other part of gut feelings involves your inner world- your emotions. In our previous example, your mind pays attention to similar situations because the original experience was significantly scary. In fact, any strong emotion associated with a novel experience will help that experience get solidified into your memory, and there it will be a constant reference point for similar situations in the future. As a reference it has not just the memories of what happened on the outside (the noise of the cracking, the vibration in the ground, the rush of air, the sight of the trunk suddenly coming down, etc.), but also the memory of the emotion. So when a similar experience is noted, your mind has it linked to the emotion and that emotion gives you a sense of what to do.

Figure out your EQ

Curious as to your EQ? Since there's no definitive test to measure EQ, what you can do is get an overall sense of your emotional intelligence. Which end of the spectrum are you closer to, or do you fall somewhere in the middle? Take some time and rate the following statements about yourself on a scale of 1-3 (1= this does not apply to me and 3= this definitely applies to me). Don't try to answer the way you wish you were, or the way you think you should answer. Just answer them as honestly as possible.

I know my own weaknesses and strengths

I can get along with most people I meet

I don't often lose my temper

I enjoy working with groups

When I get upset, I know exactly why

I'm concerned with being a good person

I can tell how people are feeling just by looking at their face

I take time out of my schedule to help people

When I fail at something it doesn't discourage me

I go with my gut feelings often

My gut feelings are often right

I am curious about new people

I'm a good leader

I can pay full attention when I need to

I can be disciplined when it is necessary

I can resist temptation

I recognize my emotions as I experience them

I can usually calm myself down when I'm upset

People tell me I'm a good listener

I set long term goals

There were 20 questions, so your score should fall somewhere between a 20 (all ones) and 60 (all threes). A score of 40 is right in the middle and anything ten points above or below means you probably have about average emotional intelligence. A score between 20 and 30 means you may not be very in touch with yours and other peoples' emotions. A score between 50 and 60 may mean that you are highly emotionally intelligent. Remember, this is just a quick way to get a sense of your own emotional intelligence at a glance. This number is not definitive, and it is not set in stone. If you want to improve your EQ, then continue reading and try some of the practices outlined in the later chapters of this book.

CHAPTER 3
APPLYING EMOTIONAL INTELLIGENCE TO YOUR LIFE

Chapter 3

Applying Emotional Intelligence To Your Life

So now you have a sense of your emotional intelligence: what you are already good at and where you may need work. Even if you scored well and feel like you have a pretty solid emotional intelligence skill set, it doesn't hurt to expand it. In fact, there are lots of reasons to make working on your EQ a priority.

How EQ Helps You and Why it's Important

What creates success in business in careers and business? The greatest factor is not IQ alone. EQ plays a huge role. There are increasingly many studies that demonstrate this. You would think that a high IQ would let you get a lot done and be very successful. Yet, very high IQ' (above 150) tend to not be very successful. All that intelligence in one area, distracts from the human element that helps you succeed in life. Relationships are important- that's what life is about.

Here are some of the ways emotional intelligence can improve your life:

Emotional intelligence can increase happiness in relationships and while alone. It can help improve discipline and willpower while decreasing those terrific highs and lows that throw your life into chaos. Emotional intelligence helps with your anger management too. In a sense you gain the ability to smooth out the emotional roller coaster life often is and gain some control in areas you might have lacked in the past.

Some of the control comes in the form of improved accountability or being aware of how much you take on yourself. Knowing your limits and how far you can push yourself keeps you from overdoing it and crashing or never going far enough.

Your honesty and trust are improved when you work on your emotional intelligence. This improvement in trust is certainly with other but also with yourself. You become able to function without resorting to white lies to get by or mistrusting everyone around you.

Your assertiveness and confidence will grow with your EQ, and this will lead to greater success at taking on new challenges. Similarly, your ability to communicate is vastly improved when you are in tune with your EQ: at work, in intimate relationships, and casual friendships you become more capable to convince people or inspire them or just make your needs clear. Along with communication your listening skills are linked to your EQ. Your ability to empathize with people and show them you understand them and reflect what they said back to them.

Something we all struggle with: stress tolerance. Yes, your EQ can have an impact on how you handle stress. Your relationships with other might be strained because of a poor ability to relate to others. You may also be increasingly stressed because of a lack of a clear understanding of yourself. Feeling frantic, judged or guilty frequently can be a sign of this.

Emotional intelligence improves your decision making. You can stop going back and forth, not being decisive, and procrastinating finally. This will give you more flexibility in life.

Of course there are always the academic studies that show academic achievement scores increase, measures of prosocial behavior go up, classroom disturbances and disruptive behavior decrease all in studies on children in classrooms who are taught some skills to improve their EQ

How to Harness Emotions for Specific Tasks

Now that we see some of the benefits of becoming better acquainted with your emotions, let's examine some of the situations our emotions can be useful to us in more detail

This does not involve getting rid of "bad" emotions and trying to have "good" ones all the time. There are intrinsic values and uses to otherwise troubling emotions we might like to avoid. You might consider it an inherent wisdom to each of these emotions, and if we can find this wisdom in each emotion, we can harness it for our own use. The emotion can help us better understand and react to a situation instead of controlling us.

We'll touch on the top three most frequently experienced emotions that are the most readily turned to your advantage.

<u>Anger</u>

Perhaps the best example of this is anger. Many of us would like to be less angry. We often do things we regret later, in anger. Yet anger still arises and there is still use and wisdom in it. The wisdom in anger is that it is an extraordinary "bullshit" detector. When we are angry, we know instinctively that we, or someone or something important to us has been wronged. There is a sense of injustice. Our expectations have been violated. Anger gives us a fast window of clarity to that wrongdoing, and it gives us something more. Anger gives us energy to do something about it. For decades, activists of all sorts have relied on anger to motivate people for this reason. It can be used as fuel.

So once you are capable of identifying that you are indeed angry, you can quickly pinpoint what it is that is wrong. Once you have that, you need only analyze the situation long enough to decide the best course of action. However, you cannot do that in the midst of anger. Anger gives you physical energy to do something- it does not provide much of a mental boost. You need to put your anger aside long enough to think critically about what you need to do. Once you have the plan clearly in mind you can return to that anger to give you the energy to see your plan through.

Fear

Fear's usefulness becomes apparent when we think about where fear (and likewise most of our emotions come from). Our ancestors needed fear, as a constant companion to help keep us alive. In fact, many animals do, just look at the squirrel outside your house. Fear is an alarm that tells us there might be problem, but there are few settings on this alarm. It is often set to maximum, which is why even small worries, like whether you will be able to make your rent on time, can set off some truly spectacular fear and worry.

The first truly great thing about fear is that it brings you down into the moment of whatever you are fearing. It heightens your senses and your mind turns to overdrive to try to solve the issue at hand. You aren't going to be very easily distracted when you are afraid. It gives you a sense of being alive, being in your body, and maybe more importantly, puts into sharp focus that which you hold dear. Whatever it is you are afraid of losing, or suffering, that you now know is something important to you. So fear can give you focus, show you what's important, and eliminate distractions.

The trick of course is learning to function within that fear, in order to use it. Fearlessness isn't "not having fear", it's acting despite fear. People often try to face fears by starting with their biggest ones, but that is a recipe for disaster. Always start small. Pick something that has minor consequences, something manageable but still fear inducing. Pay attention to what that feels like while you are experiencing the fear, and once its over, also pay attention to the relief. That relief is also partly chemical and signals your body to relax, to start digesting again, and start the immune system back up, basically to go back to normal. That aftereffect is an integral part of using the fear experience.

Happiness

We know what it is like, we know we want it, but when is the last time you thought about how to use happiness? When you are happy, the world is more inviting, you are more generous, your interactions with people are easier, more natural and problems and hiccups in your plans are minor trifles you can easily deal with. So what is the best way to use this emotion? Most of us just bask in it, enjoy it, and try to find ways to extend it and keep the emotion going. Yet, we can't exist in a state of perpetual happiness. Our mind just isn't designed for it.

Instead, you might consider using that great expansive feeling, tolerance for stress and boundless energy that comes with happiness to do something you're not actually looking forward to. That may seem counter-intuitive but think about why you don't want to do whatever it is you are avoiding? Maybe you'll struggle, and hit obstacles, or maybe its just boring. Maybe some part of it is unpleasant. These are all great reasons to use happiness to attack the problem. While in a state of happiness you are better equipped to persevere, to follow through and get past problems to get what you want. You'll be able to tolerate the stress better and maybe even joke about it.

If you think back to your experiences, you have probably done the opposite: tried to get something out of the way while you were in a bad mood. How did that work for you? Probably not that well. What's more is you can create a sense of happiness by inviting some things that make you happy to work with you: good music, a friend, a favorite drink. Whatever it is, it should be something that elevates your spirit, because that will make the difficult task all the more tolerable.

CHAPTER 4
EMOTIONAL INTELLIGENCE-SELF-IMPROVEMENT SUCCESS

Chapter 4

Emotional Intelligence -
Self-Improvement Success

We saw some examples of specific emotions being harnessed for our own advantage, but how do you know for certain what emotions you are feeling at a moment? Once you can identify them you'll need skill in controlling them and, especially important for dealing with relationships with others: being able to recognize them in other people.

How to Identify Your Emotions-

<u>Journaling</u>

It is no coincidence that some of the greatest writers in history also kept consistent journals of their daily experiences, thoughts and feelings. Journaling, specifically writing about your reflections of your experiences throughout your day, allows you to examine your feelings closely. It is important to do more than log all the events of the day. If you have never journaled before that can be a good start. However, you will want to build on that. When you write down: "Went to a movie with Jennifer", you should also include your analysis and reaction to the event. Maybe the experience was awkward when you think about it because Jennifer made some remarks about herself that you were not expecting. Or maybe the experience was entirely delightful., and you would like to repeat it.

Journaling gives you an opportunity to reflect on your life occasionally and make course adjustments. It doesn't need to be every day, so long as you are regularly thinking about what you have gone through. Physically writing it down has two major benefits: 1- Physically writing things down forces you to commit at least the time it takes to write the thoughts down, which gives you time to work through your thoughts, and if you get interrupted, you can easily begin again where you left off 2- You can take a step back and examine your thoughts. You can come back to your writings in the future and learn more about yourself by examining the thoughts of your younger self.

Meditation

We talk about meditation a little elsewhere, and you might wonder why it keeps coming up when discussing emotions. Aren't monks who pray and meditate supposed to be stoic and unfeeling? While that is a common conception, it is not entirely accurate.

The meditative practices found in many religions, yoga, and even modern mindfulness therapies all share certain characteristics that make them useful for investigating and identifying your emotions. Generally, they involve slowing down the rest of your life and giving time to focus and be mindful. This focus tends to be on one object, such as a deity, a mantra (phrase repeated over and over), an object, or often just your breath. As you focus on this one thing, you allow yourself to become mindful of what that experience is like. Without the distractions of everyday life (and this is why it is often best to start meditating in a quiet or secluded place) you will have the opportunity to notice your mind in action. As your focus is on one object only, you have the option to shift that focus momentarily and take stock of what your mind has produced.

For example, you may be sitting, focusing on your breath when all of a sudden you think that maybe the strange pain in your side is cancer. You let the thought go, focus back on the breath and suddenly remember how angry your parents will be with something you did (or failed to do) recently. You let the thought go and again your mind suddenly remembers something very important that you need to do immediately.

This is entirely typical; everyone's mind is active. In this example it also suggests an undercurrent of anxiety, as each new thought shares a trait of anxiety or worry. Since you have nothing else distracting you during the meditation you have an opportunity to notice what sort of thoughts pop into your head commonly and what sort of emotions they entail.

Meditation also allows you to check in with your body. The sitting posture most typically associated with meditation is not arbitrary: it is designed to be comfortable enough (with some practice) to allow a person to sit for prolonged periods of time, without becoming uncomfortable or needing to fidget. In this situation of calm, in a comfortable seating, you may suddenly notice a tightness in your belly for instance, that you had not noticed before while you were busily going about your day.

Your Body

We touched on this idea before, but let's explore it further now. Your body responds to each emotion and it is possible for entire clusters of emotions to be physically manifested in similar ways. For example, if your hands are suddenly sweaty, this could very likely be due to nervousness. Then again, you may also be experiencing a type of nervousness, like dread, or maybe it is full blown fear, or just low grade anxiety. For some people this can happen when relaxed or angry- and while those emotions are less frequently linked to that physiological state, that doesn't mean that it doesn't work that way for you.

Another good example is getting goosebumps. This is often associated with being scared, but for some can also be excitement. This example is particularly useful because here we can see how easy it would be to confuse these two emotions. We can think of many situations in which you would be both scared and excited: you're about to ride a roller coaster; you're about to get closer to a person you like than you have before; just before meeting someone new (maybe your palms are sweating too); even certain music can elicit this physiological response.

Listen to Music

This one may seem strange but hear me out. It's unlikely that you haven't been moved by a piece of music at some point in your life, whether it was listening to a bit of Mozart in a music appreciation class, or your favorite band in concert, or even the score of a good movie. We've all been moved by music even if we don't realize it, and indeed this is often the goal of many musicians: to elicit a certain emotion.

Studies in neuroimaging have shown that music activates brain areas that are usually associated with the experiencing of emotions. These brain areas are part of what is known as the limbic system, and exist deep within the brain. The amygdala and hippocampus work together with pathways that primarily transmit the neurotransmitter dopamine (often associated with pleasure).

So one avenue to help identify your own emotions involves examining the music you listen to. If you are having trouble figuring out how to categorize the emotional content of the music you're listening to you have a few options. First, you can simply ask friends, family and coworkers about their opinion on the artist or song you're thinking about.

If you want to do some analysis on your own, then there are certain structural features of music that tend to go hand in hand with certain associated emotions. The tempo, or speed of a piece for example can go one of two ways: fast paced and the emotion is likely somewhere near excitement or anger, whereas a slower tempo is usually linked to either sadness or a sense of peacefulness.

Some other features: The mode of music (type of scale) can indicate: either happiness in major tonality or sadness in minor tonality.

If the volume of a piece is high, it's likely intense and expressing something powerful, or angry. Something quiet might be subdued or relaxed.

The melody (this is the thing you tend to hum to yourself or get stuck in your head) might have complementing harmonies which would be associated with positive emotions like happiness or peacefulness. It may also have harmonies that clash against each other, in which case there may be a sense of excitement, anger, or even indicating something unpleasant.

The rhythm can indicate happiness or serenity through smoothness or consistency. A somewhat varied rhythm might be taken as exuberance. While an irregular rhythm could convey uneasiness.

You may also investigate your emotions by paying attention to what type of music you go to in certain situations. If you turn to heavy metal immediately after a fight with a friend or family member, we can be pretty sure there is some degree of anger involved for example.

How to Control Emotions

The first step to knowing how to control your emotions is to know when you actually need to control them. In many situations your emotional responses will be correct. When you're having a good time with your friends and you are feeling happy, there is no need to control that or do anything with the emotion. You can leave it be.

Otherwise, for each situation you can imagine needing to control your emotions, follow these steps:

-Figure out what can be modified in the situation. If there is something that is within your power, realistically to change the situation and the situation is causing your emotion (and you want to change the emotion), then it makes sense to change circumstance that you can. People run into problems when they try to change things that they don't actually have control over. You can't change another person's mind for example (though we often want to), and you can't even change their behavior (though you can hope for that more realistically). You can change your actions with a given person though.

-Shift your focus. You will notice that most emotions that really grab a hold of you, also cause your mind to shift its focus 100% on a specific thing. Your whole world shrinks to that small item, whatever it is and you lose sight of everything else. It won't be easy, but you'll find it is more possible than you think.

-Change the thoughts associated with the situation. This might be the trickiest but most effective way to gain control of your emotions. Most of the time we experience a strong emotion, it is linked to some thought or belief about how that situation will impact us. Generally positive thoughts lead to positive emotions and vice versa. The trick in changing your thoughts is that you must believe the change. If you decide a party you have to go to isn't as bad as you expect it to be, you need to really convince yourself of that before it will have any effect on your emotions.

Sometimes we can do this in a single situation when it's an easy shift or when we really need to. Usually people are really successful with this technique when they switch the thought to something very similar.

If you're hot, dehydrated and still need to walk another 15 minutes in the blazing sun you might think "This is terrible and I'm miserable", and indeed with that thought you will be miserable. You want to shift that mindset, but if you try to go 180 degrees to "This is great! I love being dehydrated!", that will never work, because you don't in fact love being dehydrated. A simpler cognitive shift might be "OK, I can do this, just another 15 minutes, that's half of an episode of my favorite show. This is doable". While you may not be suddenly joyous, if you can get on board with the slightly different thought, your mood will improve.

-Change your behavior. Studies have shown that simply smiling, even when you do not feel like smiling, can actually improve your mood. You can become happier just by pretending to be happier. The old phrases "Fake it till you make it" and "We are what we pretend to be" turn out to be more true than previously thought. This of course works for other emotions. You can gradually get your body to flow into a new emotion just by pretending you are already in that mindset.

-Beware cognitive distortions. These are ways of thinking that are very common, but nonetheless distorted ways of looking at the world that don't hold up under scrutiny. They tend to allow one emotion gain a foothold and prevent others from naturally occurring. Some examples follow:

All or nothing thinking- Seeing the world entirely in black and white categories. If something is not quite perfect for example, it's a total failure.

Overgeneralization- This is the mental habit of seeing a single event as part of a consistent pattern when it really isn't.

Mental Filter- This filter keeps everything but one detail you choose to dwell on, and that detail takes over your whole view and mindset,

Disqualifying the Good- You throw out good experiences, insist they don't count and don't allow them to influence your mood

Mind Reading- Sometimes people can guess what you are thinking, but that is all it is. When you become sure you know exactly what someone is thinking (and that thought distresses you) you've fallen into this common cognitive distortion.

Fortune Telling- Is like mind reading, in that you become convinced you know exactly how the future is going to play out. The fact is you don't, and your best guess is still just a guess, so you can let go of that belief a little.

Catastrophizing- This is taking small things in your life and blowing them up until they become end of the world scenarios. "I'm going to be homeless and alone in the world" is not the right conclusion to come to if you miss a month's rent or get a B on a test, yet some people do.

Labeling- As soon as you put a label on something or someone, you have changed the way you will think about that thing or person in the future. If you attach a very strong label, like "jerk" to a person, that will mean you will always see that person as a "jerk", even if they are not. It robs you of your chance to change your mind about things in the future

Personalization- When you see yourself as the root cause of some terrible thing, even if you were not actually responsible for it, you've fallen into this cognitive distortion.

Emotional Reasoning- Perhaps the most important distortion to be aware of if your EQ is something you are trying to work on. This is when you have an emotion and accept that emotion as a perfect reflection of the way reality actually is. Since you feel bad, things must be bad for example. If you can catch yourself doing this, you've won half the fight to controlling your emotions instead of letting them control you.

All of these ways to gain some control over your emotions will not come easily at first, especially if you are not accustomed to working with your mind. However, the more you do it, the more you practice at it, the better you will get at it. In fact, I can almost guarantee it will not always be easy. Expect some difficulty, and then when it comes, you'll be ready for it and ready to keep going and persevere through it.

How to Read Emotions in Others

This is perhaps one of the most difficult skills to learn in this entire book if you are working on building your emotional intelligence. It really requires that you have first examined yourself and have been able to identify your own emotions in numerous situations. Without that basic understanding of human emotions that you gain from firsthand experience, you will be forced to learn about other peoples' emotions in a totally different way: more like a math problem than something you can incorporate into your daily intuition.

So assuming you've done your homework and learned a little about emotions from yourself, let's dive into the way to help you read another person's emotions

The Sound of Communication

This is important because the way someone says something can completely change the meaning of what they are saying and convey radically different emotions. Take the simple phrase: "Oh, isn't that nice?". If you imagine a kind old grandparent saying that while watching their grandchildren play, you get one emotion: likely happiness. If you imagine a disgruntled looking boss standing with arms folded looking down on a pair of his employees slacking on the job, you get a totally different emotion: annoyance, frustration or even anger conveyed through sarcasm.

Tone is the type of attitude that is behind the words a person uses. Related to tone is the pitch a person uses when talking. This is basically the ups and downs in the sound of their voice. If it is flat and unchanging they may be bored, yet if unchanging and flat and it seems forces, the person may be actively trying not to express some other emotion.

Within the verbal aspect of a person's speech, there is also the rate at which a person talks: quick might show excitement while slow might indicate a lower energy mood like relaxation or sadness. What if the speed is normal but there are many pauses? This might be an indicate some trouble finding the right words, or some trouble expressing something important or personally relevant. If the topic is that important there is likely an emotion linked to it.

Facial Expressions

This is a difficult aspect of emotions to learn through text, or to try to learn at once. It's something that most people learn slowly over the course of their entire lifetimes, but it is something you can learn to develop if you pay attention. The trick to speed up your learning is to know where exactly on the face to look when trying to assess emotions.

The human face has numerous muscles that can contract to produce hundreds of novel combinations, yet certain combinations related to specific emotions are quite common, even across cultures across the world. We'll go through a few here.

.Happiness:

We all know a smile when we see it, but there is a difference between genuine happiness and a forces smile. The difference is in the crinkle at the corners of the outside of the eyes. This is an involuntary muscle contraction that indicates genuine pleasure. When you see someone smile without any trace of an eye crinkle, you can be sure the smile is for the benefit of others and not a true representation of their emotional state.

Anger:

Anger tends to involve a furrowing of the brows: the eyebrows come down as if trying to meet at a point between the eyes, shading the eyes and wrinkling the skin between them. At the same time the eyes seem to widen or bulge as the eyelid pulls back. The muscle just under the eye might even contract noticeably. More extreme anger might involve the upper lip curling back to expose the teeth or noticeable jaw and teeth clenching. The nostrils often flare (widen out) unconsciously as well.

Sadness:

Often in sadness the lower lip will protrude as the jaw pulls up and closes. The eyebrows tend to pull up and toward a middle point above the brows, pushing together, but raised and wrinkling the center of the forehead. More extreme sadness on the verge of tears will crinkle the eyes (as you might notice in genuine happiness) in addition to the other features.

How to Use EQ in a Given Situation

Using your EQ in any given situation is going to rely on your ability to assess the situation and pick and choose from your skill set. There is no one simple rule that applies to all situations (though we might wish there were).

Instead, we can offer you a couple of simple techniques that will help you activate your emotional intelligence in any given situation. Some of our biggest blunders come in times when we react too quickly without really considering the situation from the emotional side (or sometimes we consider the situation entirely from the emotional side in an uncontrolled and chaotic way). To avoid these common pitfalls, you need a way to activate those parts of your brain that handle your emotional intelligence. Here are a couple:

Check-ins

Elsewhere in this book we touch on the idea of automatic thoughts that lead to emotions and how you can gain insight into your emotions by learning to pay attention to those automatic thoughts. In any given situation you can employ a similar technique of checking-in. The first check-in you should always do is one about how you are feeling in the moment. Knowing what you are feeling in a moment gives you insight into what direction your impulses are leading you to and whether you want to go in that direction.

Let's say for example your boss gives you instructions that just don't make sense (I'm sure that's never happened to you, but let's pretend). After a while you have about had it with the task and want to say something sarcastic to your boss about it. This would be a good time for a quick check-in with your emotions. Are you feeling frustrated with the task? Has it made you angry, and does that anger make you want to act? Seems like it, but is insulting your boss the best use of your energy? Probably not. So what should you do instead?

This is where part two the check-in comes in: stop for a moment and try to imagine what the other person is feeling. In this example you haven't seen your boss for some time, while you worked on the frustrating task. It's likely your boss will not be in a bad mood (unless he/she is also having a bad day), and will not appreciate that you have reason to be upset. Imagining what your boss might think of you is taking it yet another step further, using the theory of mind to help you out. He/she probably has no idea that the task was poorly designed, but at the same time, few people response well to sarcasm or outright anger.

So what should you do instead? First take the useful part of your frustration and anger: it's energy to make you want to do something to change the situation. Next remember that your boss will not know why you are upset, nor will he/she appreciate rudeness. So, in expressing your frustration you want to do so in a way that makes them want to listen. You could say something like: "Do you think there might be a better way to do this? I've been doing this for a while and I see some problems here and there." Allow your boss time to get to your level, to realize there is a problem and to decide a solution is needed. Too many people start by offering the solution before the other person even knows why they're speaking at all. Keeping in mind where the other person's mind is at is crucial to effective communication and good communication is what allows you to get what you need from other people.

Discernment without Judgment

This may seem like a strange idea because the concepts are so similar. Both involve a sense of being able to tell one thing apart from another. Yet they have a very important difference. Judgment involves a sense of moral right and wrong, a sort of conclusion about the goodness of something. Think of a judge in a court who must decide based on all the facts and testimonies the final fate of the people or situation in question. Not only does the judge have to tease everything apart and understand it, the judge must come to a final conclusion that we would tend to see as good or bad depending on our involvement.

Discernment on the other hand involves a similar process of discriminating between one thing and another, but lacks that final moral judgment When you discern something without judgment you don't come to that final conclusion about whether it is good or bad. Often we discern things in our environment very quickly first and then almost a quickly come to an immediate snap judgment

For example, you are forced to go into work or school on a day you don't normally come in. Discernment involves being able to see all the logistics of such a situation such as: how you need to change your routine for that day, what errands you need to reschedule, how much time you need to give to work or school, the difference in pay or your final grade that it will mean, the loss of your free time. All the minutia of the situation are broken down and understood for their impacts.

Judgment in a situation like this would be something like: "Ugh, this is terrible. I can't believe I have to give up my Saturday. My day is ruined." Or even "This is great! My paycheck at the end of the week is going to be so much higher because of this extra day". Both are final judgments, or conclusions about the situation based on your ability to discern the problems and opportunities that arise from it. Those judgments come with them a sense of the goodness or badness of a situation. A sense of the desirableness. That sense will inform your emotions. If the extra time at work or school is terrible, you will feel angry, sad, annoyed or frustrated about the whole situation. If that extra time is great, then you will be happy, excited, even energetic to go about your day.

Since those judgments inform what kind of emotion we will have about a situation it is a skillful practice of your emotional intelligence to be able to watch them and even question them. These judgments happen very quickly, often automatically and without our conscious input, so don't get hung up trying to prevent them in the first place. That would be like trying to prevent your emotions from happening at all- which would be unrealistic and unhealthy.

Instead, just as you check in with what you are feeling, and what the other person seems to be feeling in a situation, check in with your judgment of it as well. Is that judgment sound? Can you look at the situation without coming to that final conclusion? Can you see all the pros and cons and wait on passing any judgment? The more you engage in this kind of practice, the more readily your mind will think about these issues, and more easily grapple with them. Like any skill, what is hard and awkward at first will become fluid, easier and perhaps even second nature with practice.

CHAPTER 5

EMOTIONAL INTELLIGENCE-
RELATIONSHIP SUCCESS WITH OTHERS

Chapter 5

Emotional Intelligence -
Relationship Success With
Others

The previous chapter have focused in large part on the "how" and "why" of working with your own emotions. Remember the core parts of Emotional Intelligence from Chapter 1? Those are the first two core concepts. Now let's look at the remaining core concepts that deal more with other people, their emotions and how to be successful in your interactions with others.

Social Skills

Social skills are any behaviors that facilitate the way you interact with other people. Even if it is in a one on one setting, you need some social skills to effectively communicate with other people. Each culture and group of people will have their own set of rules, generally unwritten to help people interact with each other effectively.

These skills may not be immediately obvious because we use so many of them every day. Even something as small as ordering a cup of coffee in the morning involves a number of social skills: Waiting in line, respecting other people's boundaries, not staring at people, yet making good eye contact with the person you are talking to, talking at the right volume, smiling or cracking a joke at the right time to make someone else laugh or smile, using pleasantries, politeness.

Not everyone will possess the same range or breadth of these skills. Some people will excel in some areas and be weak in others. However, social skills are also very situational. The skills required to interact with others in one setting may not be sufficient in another. Fora example the skills needed to interact favorably with college students in a club at midnight are not entirely the same set of skills needed for a glamorous upscale ball. While much of the difference might be etiquette, the ability to discern where one type of etiquette is needed is another social skill.

Generally, people develop enough social skills through the years to get by. One can consciously study and pay attention to the social interactions of others to try to improve, but for most people's needs, that is unnecessary. Usually your mind is updating your social skill set automatically by noting what other people in your environment are doing. However, every time we move into a new place, situation, geographic location or even neighborhood, we will want to supplement that unconscious attention with our own keen awareness.

Building Empathy

Empathy is the ability to feel the feelings another person is most likely having. Basically, it's the ability to put yourself in someone else's shoes. When someone else is in pain, physical or emotional, you empathize when you have some understanding of what it is like to experience that pain. Though we most often associate empathy with the experience of pain, as well as concepts like compassion and sympathy which also involve the suffering of others, empathy goes beyond this one dimension. Another example of empathy would be hearing a person's story of being unjustly wronged and feeling the anger that they might also be feeling. Empathy encompasses the whole range of emotional experiences.

As with other human qualities, some people will be naturally more empathic and some less so. As we've mentioned earlier, emotional understanding can help you in work, social, academic and interpersonal situations. As such, it pays to try to develop your understanding of other people's emotions. It will benefit you in your dealings with others, but it will also benefit others, as they feel validated by your understanding.

Read more

This one may not be obvious at first but the more you do it, the more you will notice the benefit. We're talking about works of fiction or nonfiction that deal primarily with people and their interactions. Reading more popular science articles, news, self-help, or technical articles will not help you learn to understand other people and their emotions better. Literature that deals with people, the kind that portrays people and their emotions, their struggles, their behaviors and motivations gives us a window into what is called "theory of mind". Knowing that someone else has emotions is one thing, but being able to understand what they might be thinking requires some experience with similar situations and you can build that experience without actually being there. Books can act as a proxy for those situations, and so long as your mind is paying attention to what you are reading and working through the material, trying ti understand it, you will benefit from it.

Active listening

There is a difference to listening to music while you work out and listening to someone give you directions. In one you aren't really paying attention to what you are hearing, and in the other you are paying very close attention. Active listening is the latter example. It involves completely tuning yourself into whatever it is you are listening to. This means actively ignoring distractions and focusing on what or who you are listening to.

Much of human communication goes beyond words. You've probably noticed how easily you can misunderstand someone's words through a text or email. The words themselves are only a fraction of the total meaning being communicated. When speaking with others their tone, their body language, their facial expressions, their volume, all play a part in conveying the meaning of what they are expressing. When you only give part of your attention to someone you miss many of these other cues and you can easily draw incorrect conclusions about what they are saying. More so, they feel your lack of attention and interest, and will feel more distant from you, which makes future honest communication more difficult.

How can you tell if you are not actively listening? Are you checking your phone? Are you reading a menu, checking an email, or fidgeting with your clothes or accessories? If you are doing any of these things, your attention is not fully on the person you are supposed to be listening to. What about your mind? Are you thinking about what you are going to do later in the day? Or about an anxiety at work or discomfort at the moment, or a joke you just can't wait to tell? If your mind is somewhere else than the person in front of you then you are not actively listening.

One way to check in with your active listening is to try "simple repeats". Every now and then, when appropriate in the conversation try to repeat what you have heard, but in your own words. If someone is telling you about all the things they want to do this weekend now that they have their paycheck you might say "So you're really excited to spend your pay and can't decide on what you want to do?" This way you can check on your understanding and the person you are talking to will feel validated in being understood.

Meditation

Since your mind can get in the way of listening to someone, you can improve your ability to actively listen (and therefore your empathy) by practicing some type of meditation. Being able to work with your mind, and having practice quieting it, or at least being familiar enough with it that you can recognize when your attention is drifting will help you really connect with another person.

Another advantage of meditation is that is gives a sort of laboratory to experiment with and observe your thoughts. As you meditate seemingly random thought s will appear frequently. They say the human mind produces around

50,000 thoughts per day. Yet, these thoughts are not all random. Many of them will follow several themes important to your life. As you meditate you can begin to notice the categories these thoughts fall into, what themes they fit and you can gradually learn about how your mind works. As you learn how your mind works, you will gain deeper understanding of others. We are after all, more alike than we are different.

Being present with pain/suffering

This one is hard. It's something we often do not want to do, but is part of what we would call compassion, and compassion and empathy are closely tied. Often we tend to avoid exposing ourselves to someone else's pain or misfortunes (unless we really dislike that person), and we do that out of a natural empathy. But we are only touching the surface by avoiding it. There are deeper and more complex emotions beyond the surface pain. If you can abide by the suffering of another long enough, you can find those other emotions that they are experiencing and struggling with. You may find those experiences useful in your own times of pain, or you may gain a greater understanding of the person in front of you. In any event, that person will appreciate your ability to be with them and will open your relationship to more genuine and honest communication.

This doesn't mean go find a random person in a hospital bed and sit with them. Everyone has their own problems, pains, and emotional struggles. To each person these are real, serious, and a big part of their reality. Just because you might think the problem is small or inconsequential, does not mean the other person does. You can see this most clearly with small children who might for example weep over dropping an ice cream cone. That pain is real to them. You might try practicing with someone in a similar situation: with a problem that is bearable for you but troubling for them and slowly build up your tolerance for more difficult situations. As you do, you will be increasing your comfort zone with other people, meaning you will be able to interact with more people, understand them better and accomplish more in your own life through that understanding and improved relationships.

<u>Build your own self-awareness of emotions</u>

How can you know what someone else is feeling if you don't even understand how you feel in a given situation? To practice this, you can take a page out of the books of Cognitive Behavioral Therapy (CBT). CBT therapy asks people to question their thoughts regularly, especially what they call "automatic thoughts". These are the thoughts that immediately precede an emotion. For example, you might find yourself often getting upset and not knowing why exactly. You would ask yourself: "What was I just thinking". It will be difficult at first to catch yourself quickly enough to notice the thought, but there is an important, though fleeting thought that leads to the emotion.

Let's say your spouse tells you their parents are coming tomorrow for a surprise visit. Maybe you get upset and ask yourself just as soon as you notice you're getting upset: "Why am I getting upset? What was I just thinking?". You rewind your mind a moment and realize the very first thing that popped into your head, without you purposefully thinking it was something like "Oh no, this is going to suck". You write that down and look at the sentence. Then you can ask yourself, "Why do I think this is going to suck?". Generally, there is some underlying belief about a situation or even all of reality that prompts these unbidden thoughts. Being able to catch them, and challenge their assumptions gives you freedom from the initial thought and the emotion it began.

<u>Test your hypothesis</u>

This is similar to the previously mentioned "simple repeats" but can be more direct. Ask someone how they are feeling if it is appropriate- Example- someone just told you no one listened to them at work, and their car broke down, and they can't find their phone, you might say: "It sounds like you had a rough day. You must be pretty frustrated right now" If that's not what they're feeling they'll explain their emotions and you get more feedback and information to work with in the future. If it is what they are feeling you can pat yourself on the back for guessing right and then talk to them about that feeling, and what they need to feel better.

CONCLUSION

Conclusion

Thank you again for downloading this book!

I hope this book was able to help you to understand your own emotions and develop your emotional intelligence. As we mentioned, your emotional intelligence is the key to not only understanding yourself and others, but through that understanding follow through on your goals and aspirations more effectively.

The next step is to start practicing what you learned in your day to day life. You can't learn a new skill and expect it to stay fresh and strong without some practice. Take your newfound emotional intelligence into the trenches of your everyday interactions. Use it to help you deal with your boss and coworkers more effectively. Use it to understand your friends better and deepen those relationships. Use it just for fun with a stranger or new acquaintance. Each interaction enriches your life and deepens your abilities.

Part of this next step is to make continually improving emotional intelligence a routine part of your life. The key to any good routine is starting small, and persistence. Take just one suggestion from this book, whether it's journaling, or meditation, or practicing active listening., and make it something you commit to doing regularly. Make your initial goals, small and achievable.

Finally, if you enjoyed this book, please take the time to share your thoughts and post a review on Amazon. It'd be greatly appreciated!

Thank you and good luck!

Your Free Gift

As a way of saying thanks for your purchase, Aya has made a Free companion to this book that will help you get results with regards to your purpose, finances, health and many more using the power of affirmations. Get excited, enthusiastic, and live a more fulfilling life with: *101 Affirmations Companion Guide*.

This PDF has **actionable and easy to do techniques** in a printable checklist to get the results you want.

http://bit.ly/affirmpdf

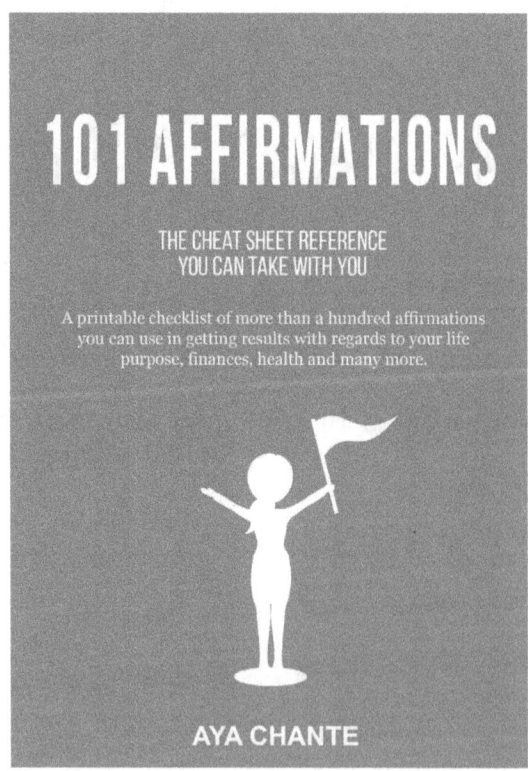

www.ingramcontent.com/pod-product-compliance
Lightning Source LLC
Chambersburg PA
CBHW060224290526
45789CB00003B/1395